The Cure for Writer's Block

Special thanks to my parents.

The
CURE
for
WRITER'S
BLOCK

ANDREW MAYNE

Contents

Diagnosing Writer's Block

Writer's Block is a simple term that covers a lot of different situations. I wrote this guide because the #1 question I get when I talk about writing is, how do you cure writer's block? When I ask people to describe what they're trying to fix, the symptoms break down into three different kinds of writer's block. I define them as follows:

Writer's Blank: When you want to write something and be creative, but don't know what story to tell. You're literally looking at a blank page with no idea how to begin.

Writer's Lock: When the ideas are there, but you don't know how to make them coalesce. You're unsure of where to begin and how to tell the story.

Writer's Knot: The story, the conflict and the characters are all there, but you're stuck in the middle. This is when you're trying to navigate your way through the fog and keep running into things.

My goal with this guide is to explain the strategies that have worked well for me in dealing with these situations. Hopefully, if you're in the middle of writing something right now, you won't even have to finish this book. You'll find some inspiration and be able to quickly jump right into your story.

On the subject of inspiration, let's start with Writer's Blank, and where ideas come from...

Opening Night

In downtown Hollywood, a few blocks away from the world famous Grauman's Chinese Theatre, there's a live musical that's been playing every Friday night since 1998.

I'm not a much of a musical fan, but I've been to dozens of shows and every single time I see *Opening Night* I'm thoroughly entertained. The jokes are great, the songs are hilarious and the choreography wonderfully fills the small stage. It's an hour of pure fun.

Why do I bring this up?

Because *Opening Night* is completely improvised.

The plot, the dialog, the songs and the dance numbers are made up on the spot based on suggestions from the audience. The cast wings the whole thing from start to finish every show.

This isn't just a single improv sketch performed until the actors find a punchline, it's a complete narrative with a beginning, middle and ending. There are character arcs and a resolution that comes as a surprise (often appropriately and ridiculously.)

In all the times I've seen the show, the actors have never called a time out or stopped the play to figure out what happens next. The show keeps going. Sure, it helps to have a cast of people ready to jump in and advance the story, but often you can see that so many creative possibilities have been set up that the real challenge is not chasing after them all.

How do the cast of *Opening Night* and other performers of long form improv do what they do?

While it probably helps to be born with the genetic gift of a great singing voice and whatever genes help with a quick wit, they're able to do what they do because of experience.

They understand character and conflicts. They get dramatic structure. They know all the gimmicks for creating catchy songs. They've seen hundreds of plays and practiced making things up on the spot so many times they can do it in real-time.

The cast of *Opening Night* is able to take one idea, just two or three words, and spin them into an hour of entertainment.

If you want to do the math, that's equal to about 10,000 written words or 40 pages of a paperback they create on the spot then throw away as the lights fade sixty minutes later.

Put that way, it sounds superhuman.

It's not.

It's a skill.

And the best part of this skill is that it can be learned and grown. Anyone can learn to be a better improviser.

Understanding where ideas come from and how to improvise on the keyboard means you can always keep the show going.

Fun fact: I once saw a wonderful spontaneous magic show and congratulated the performers afterwards. I mentioned Opening Night and they both gave me a knowing look. It turns out the magicians, Dave Cox and Bill Chott, were founding members of the show.

Writer's Blank:

How to find the right story

Storytelling is in your DNA

540,000 years ago a precursor to modern man, Homo Erectus (upright man), picked up a mollusk shell and carved a series of grooves on its surface. Half a million years later, Homo Sapiens, inhabiting a cave in France, painted epic illustrations on the walls of the great beasts they hunted and the world they lived in.

Why?

To know the precise answer we would have to travel back in time and ask them.

But for a general answer, we can ask someone a little more contemporary: You.

Let's travel back in time to when you were five years old and watch as you sit down at the kitchen table with a box of Crayons and a blank sheet of paper.

If you're like most five-year-olds, you're going to draw stick figures of your family (probably with distorted features – because you're thinking far more abstractly than you do now.) You'll make drawings of your pets, your friends, your house. Maybe you will also draw your favorite characters, Batman, Wonder Woman, R2-D2.

But you probably also drew things happening. Was your family holding hands? Is your dog chasing a ball? Are there villains in your drawing?

In many of your drawings there was some kind of conflict – an event that threatened to disrupt things for better or worse. This conflict could have been something real, a trip to the movies, something sad, moving away, or something you imagined entirely. You intuitively grasped that a story involved change.

Now let's travel to just night. You're watching yourself sleep. Creepy, I know. At several points in the night you dreamed. Even if you don't remember it, your brain entered into a REM state and pulled up a variety of images and symbols from your unconscious and played them out before you.

Maybe the dreams had meaning. Often they're just random data dumps. But we've all had at least some dreams where there was a sense of structure and some inherit conflict that we or the person we were observing was trying to resolve.

When your friend asks you what you did the other day, the details and observations you give are your own brand of storytelling. Do you focus on the tiny details? Only talk about the fun parts? Even people who experience the same event will relate it differently, not inaccurately, but with various points of view and insight. These choices are part of your personal touch.

All of these examples are meant to prove a point: You don't become a storyteller. You are a storyteller. You were a storyteller before you were born. You're part of a species that succeeded despite incredible odds because of your ability to transmit abstract information, share learned experiences and communicate across time and space.

Within your mind is a built-in tool that can create narratives. It even works when you're asleep. The key is to understand how to apply it, from carving patterns into shells on the beach to sitting down in front of a keyboard and taking the swirling maelstrom of thoughts in your head and organizing them in the form of words.

Summing it up: Storytelling is something you already do naturally.

Try this: Think of all the times you've told a story, verbally relaying something that happened or through other means, like selecting photos for an album. What are your natural instincts for story?

The Story Formula

Let me tell you a story. It's really short. Here we go:

1 + 2 = 3

Isn't it riveting?

Okay, maybe not. I didn't say it was a good story, but technically it had all the elements for a story. There were characters and or events: 1, 2 and 3. There was a conflict: We were adding 1 plus 2 to get the plot. This was forcing a change on the current state of events. There was a resolution: 1 plus 2 turned out to be 3.

What if we substitute the elements of the story with something else? Let's use a little algebra and change the numbers to variables.

A + B = C

This story isn't quite as clear because the letters are abstract representations of things we haven't described yet.

What if A represented a person and B was an event?

(nun) + (robs a bank) = C

C is the outcome of that event. It's the product of the conflict. It could be:

- Goes to jail

- Saves orphanage

- Becomes a crime boss

- Saves the orphanage, goes to jail and becomes a mobster.

Your job as a storyteller, and to be honest, the fun part of the job, is to figure out all the little details. Why did she do it? What choices did she make? Who was trying to stop her? Who helped her? What would be the proper outcome?

Most stories are little more complex with more variables than 1 + 2 = 3 (hopefully), but the math is the same. Something happens to something and there's an outcome. Sometimes things change for the better. Sometimes for the worse. Other times they go back to the way they were before.

We can make the formula a little more clear:

Character + Conflict = Story

Every story is based on this formula. Even ones that don't involve people. A character is anything that can experience change. It can be a nun or a tectonic plate merging into another forming a subcontinent.

Anything that doesn't follow that formula is just a description, little more than an encyclopedia entry.

What makes a story compelling is the choices you make and the way you tell it. These are all subjective decisions.

We could take our 1 + 2 = 3 example and substitute some slightly more sophisticated numbers and expressions and keep a mathematician on the edge of their seat. You and I might not be as engrossed.

On the other hand, you could have an absolutely fascinating conflict and a character that's no more interesting than our number 1, and have a story that falls flat on its face. You could have a great character, a brilliant conflict and a resolution that doesn't make any sense and people will put your book down in confusion, just as if you wrote 1 + 2 = Penguin. The few that either love the absurd or thrive on making imaginary leaps may decide you're a genius. (There is an entire sub-genre of bizarro literature...) Mileage may vary.

There are countless different story formulas, but they all involve the idea of change. Things change in a story. Your job is to figure out the things and imagine the change.

Summing it up: A story is how conflict causes change.

Try this: Think of your favorite stories and identify the conflicts. What was the condition of the world and the characters at the start? What changed at the end?

What it Means to Write What You Know

If we were to walk down the aisle of a bookstore and glance at the titles on the shelves, we'd see stories ranging from mundane personal memoirs to galaxy-spanning space opera. The characters might range from quiet shopkeepers to immortal vampires.

Peering past the wide variety of topics, and examining the authors of these stories, we'd realize that they all have something in common – even the ones telling the most exotic high fantasy; they're writing from their experiences.

You never have to visit Oz to tell the story of a teenage girl that finds herself magically transported there. But it does help to know something about courage, the determined resolve of a young woman and the kinds of imaginative characters we'd find interesting.

When you're told to write what you know, it doesn't mean that you should only write what you know about. It means that you should start with your own experiences and examples and then add to them your interests, your passions and questions you've always been wanting to ask.

J.K. Rowling, to my knowledge, has never been to the Wizarding World, but she had firsthand experience in English schools and was even a head girl. The grounded parts of the Harry Potter series, taking place in an academic environment, were based on her personal experiences. She added in a fascination for magic and her personal sense of whimsy to create a modern classic.

Your stories, all of them, are going to be based in part on your experiences. While the conflicts might be totally invented, the details, large parts of the DNA that make up the story, should come from things you've already experienced.

You could take the experience of disagreeing with a friend and place it in a restaurant or on the bridge of a space ship at the far end of the solar system. Or you could just invent a conflict from whole cloth based on what you know about human nature. But if you have real examples, why not use them? There are probably a thousand more details there than you may realize at first thought. Mine them. Paint them. Twist them. Use them as the building blocks of your story.

What kind of stories should you write?

Short answer: Anything you want.

Long answer: Stories based or influenced by your experiences, interests and passions.

Experience: What you have firsthand knowledge about (your jobs, your family, your friends, your world.)

Interests: Things you are knowledgeable about (hobbies, topics, history, anything.)

Passions: The things you are curious about (love, conflict, things you want to become more knowledgeable about.)

People who insist that you have to possess firsthand knowledge about everything you write are full of it. Yes, there is no substitute for experience, but any well-developed story is going to be filled with dozens of characters and situations that would be impossible for any one person to have experienced. That's why it's your job as a writer to do your research, use your imagination and develop your storytelling skills to fill in the gaps.

It's often the case that people who are too close to something may not appreciate what a reader might. The writer exists to observe and communicate this.

Summing it up: Your experiences can form the foundation of your story. Your stories don't have to be literally based on them, but can draw depth from your human experience. As a writer, you have complete license to embellish and changes things however you please. You're not only paid to lie, it's a requirement.

Try this: Think of some life experiences and how you could use them as a starting point to a story. What if there had been a monster at that boring summer camp you went to? What if a blind date turned out to be a wanted criminal? Start with what you know, then make up the rest.

Mining Your Experiences

Have a seat right there. Excuse me while I turn on this light and shine it in your eyes. What? It's too bright. Sorry, can't be helped. This is an interrogation. I need you to focus on your answers and not the man behind the desk.

We're going to take an inventory of your life, starting with your childhood, up until the moment the van pulled up and you were dragged inside and brought here.

Start with your earliest memory. What is it? Where were you born? Why were you born? Did your parents plan you or were you a delightful surprise? Where did you go to school? Who were your friends? What was your first job? What were the circumstances around your first kiss? Ever flown a plane? A kite?

I could go on, but my point here is that I could ask you an endless number of questions and you're going to have unique answers for all of them. The more you explore your experiences, the more corridors and rooms you'll discover.

As a writer, you want to mine this information and find those precious gems that you can use in your stories.

You don't have to have a particularly interesting life to tell a fascinating experience. In fact, often the best stories are about very ordinary people with mundane lives that have an extraordinary experience.

Your boring life sitting at a desk doing call support would be suddenly not so boring if one of your callers said they were about to kill somebody and you had to talk them out of it.

The extreme nature of the situation would be grounded with the realism you're familiar with. Remember my example of a former head girl in an English school using that as a foundation for the adventures of a boy wizard...

Summing it up: The more you mine your own experiences, the more you'll find opportunities for storytelling.

Try this: Write down as many experiences, interests and passions you have. If you put them on notecards, you can arrange them and look for interesting combinations. Throw in some wild card, What if..., questions, and you'll never run out of ideas. Your job will be to pick the good ones.

Here's a list of starter questions for your cards:

- Jobs you've had

- Places you've been

- Interesting people you've met

- Jobs you wanted

- Horrible things that have happened

- Wonderful things that have happened

- Family members

- Family member occupations

- Friends

- Friend occupations

- Enemies

- Strangest experiences

- Favorite experiences

- Where you've lived

- Schools you've attended

- Clubs and organizations you've belonged to

- Hobbies

- Types of books you read

As I pointed out, just because your answers are from the point of view of a 21st Century person living in a normal world, that doesn't mean you can't apply these experiences to a wide variety of stories.

Vampires often have to get jobs and pay rent. People in the future will still have to deal with a lot of the same personal drama that you and I experience.

Think of these experiences as building blocks. Your story is what you make from them.

Finding Stories

While the details of your story can be drawn from your own experiences, sometimes we have to reach outside ourselves for the overarching plot or premise. We might have all the right elements; great characters, interesting personal conflicts, but we're missing the narrative arc that ties them all together.

If you're a thriller or mystery writer, you don't have to look any further than headline news.

When Peter Benchley read a story about a shark hunter harpooning a two-ton Great White off the coast of Long Island, New York, he found a catalyst for his lifelong fascination with sharks and elements of the fisherman who would later become immortalized in the character of Quint in *Jaws*.

Ian Fleming's Naval Intelligence Division experiences in World War II and the various characters he encountered, spies, commandos and even his own brother, inspired the creation of James Bond.

Michael Crichton took developments in the field of genetics and (possibly inspired by the controversy over the book *In His Own Image*; David Rorvik's so-called true story of a millionaire who finances a secret project to produce a clone) created the story of a theme park filled with dinosaurs going awry in *Jurassic Park*.

Gillian Flynn's *Gone Girl*, which became an amazing film directed by David Fincher from a screenplay by Flynn, revolves around a case that feels like something CNN's Nancy Grace would spend weeks covering in minute detail.

If you look around, you'll find countless starting points for stories. As a fiction writer, you can use these as influences, but provide your own spin on them.

Part of why *Gone Girl* works so well as a thriller is that the case of the missing wife feels so similar to a real event, but because this is a work of fiction, Flynn gets to use our expectations and biases against us.

Jaws and *Jurassic Park* made compelling books and films because their subjects, a shark with a vengeance and dinosaurs brought back to life, are almost science fiction, but so close to reality that we as an audience feel like they could happen, which makes the drama all the more realistic.

Your next conflict could be today's headline or meme. Here's a list of places to go looking for them:

News: What are the big stories of the day? What are the little ones? Every day the local news crime blotter recounts events dramatically affecting the lives of at least one person.

History: Our past is filled with incredible events that shaped the world we live in. All too often the lives of the little people are forgotten, whether they're the foot soldiers that served the great leaders, or the millions of individuals that had their lives torn apart by war. There are so many stories that haven't been told, that should.

Museums: Take a trip to local museum or historical attraction and start talking to the guides. They'll fill your heads with more stories and conflicts than you could imagine.

Interviews: Stephen Ambrose's interviews with the surviving members of Easy Company formed the basis for his book and the HBO series, *Band of Brothers*. These incredible tales of heroism were just waiting for someone to come and ask about them. What would you find out interviewing local cops, firefighters or school teachers?

There's no need to be shy about it. Just call someone up, tell them you're writing a book and show up with a recorder.

Science: If you keep up with the latest events in science, you'll find countless jumping off points to wonderful 'What if?' scenarios. From viral epidemics to radical new cures that carry with them new ethical considerations, science is filled with intriguing possibilities and fascinating personalities.

Summing it up: The world is filled with story possibilities that grow much faster than the number of writers seeking inspiration. Nearly everything you read called 'news' has some story angle that can be mined.

Try this: Pick up a newspaper (while you can) and circle all of the possible story ideas you can find. It might be something sensational, such as a murder case or something mundane, but with great personal stakes like a school board election.

Writing Prompts

So you've strip-mined your past, combed today's news and gaslighted everyone you know in search of literary gold and still haven't found something.

The problem could be that you're being too picky. You're still looking for the "perfect" story, instead of just a good one. The trouble is that perfect rarely announces itself. It's usually disguised as "good" or "might be interesting."

You might be too choosy because you lack confidence in your own ideas. Guess what? We all do. That's why your job is to just pick something that at least on the surface has the potential to be good.

If you're still in this situation, I suggest a writing prompt. This is a starting point for a story where you fill in the blanks.

As a rule, I think writing prompts are a good way to practice your story weaving capabilities, but if you find that you constantly need them, then maybe your head isn't full of ideas trying to escape. Harper Lee only had to prove her worth with just one book! In my personal experience, most of the really great authors I know don't have trouble dreaming up stories. Maybe they started with some difficulty, but after they learned how to release their creativity, their problem is finding the time to bring them all to fruition. Story prompts are training wheels. The sooner you get off them, the better off you'll be.

That said, here are a number of ways you can generate somewhat random ideas for stories.

Writing Prompts

Look up "Writing prompts" on Google. You'll find a number of examples. Like this gem (which I've altered to protect the innocent: "Despite the fact that Jill ate all the pie, Lisa couldn't get herself too angry about it." Or a random sequence of words: "Picnic basket, car crash, stripper pole, drinking fountain, unicorn."

What and why?

This is so much better than writing prompts, because all the elements are coming from your twisted brain. Just take any event, headline or thought that crosses your brain and ask 'What if?' and then put something after it.

This could be something bonkers: What if Ben Franklin fought vampires?

Something mundane: What if a teacher never learned to read?

Something messed up: What if your letter carrier was reading your mail?

These kinds of prompts can lead to some very interesting places. After you ask 'What?' your next step is to ask 'Why?' a lot and then 'What?' again.

Why is your letter carrier reading your mail? What happens when you find out? The 'Why' is the heart of the story. This is the part you show us in your writing. The 'Why' could be sinister or it could be something else. Maybe the letter carrier is trying to protect you? Maybe she thinks you're a terrorist? Maybe she's in love with you!

Twist things

Most stories can be reduced to several basic plots. Spy movies can be reduced to two: A renegade spy from the agency is now the bad guy. Or our hero is now being hunted by his former spy agency. That's basically every *Mission: Impossible* movie and half the recent James Bond movies. What makes them interesting is in how they're told and the choices that are made.

You can create something fresh by taking something familiar and putting a new twist on it. This can be just changing up the characters or the outcome.

With the *The Twilight Saga*, Stephanie Meyers took a familiar genre, paranormal romance, which Anne Rice had been doing for years, and set it in a high school. Probably the most improbable place for a vampire to hang out (outside Sunnyvale, at least) but a great environment to tell stories to a teen audience.

E.L. James, a passionate *Twilight* fan-fiction writer, wrote a story about Bella and Edward having a very adult and er, kinky, relationship, then took away all the vampire elements, leaving behind the other stuff and created *50 Shades of Grey*. A huge financial success and fan favorite, if not a literary one (which could be said about *Twilight*.)

The Magicians by Lev Grossman is like Harry Potter, only the students attend college, have sex and get high – much like a real college. He took a very familiar story and asked, "What if they were like real college kids?"

Change the POV

Sometimes all it takes to come up with a great story is just to shift the point of view. In *Wicked*, Gregory Maguire gave us a sympathetic portrait of the Wicked Witch of the West from the *Wizard of Oz*. Maguire was able to use this character in his story because the original book is now in the public domain – whereas

E.L. James had to change her Edward and Bella to other characters in *Fifty Shades of Grey*.

The character of Dexter Morgan, from Jeff Lindsay's novel *Darkly Dreaming Dexter*, is a serial killer and the protagonist. Although books like Patricia Highsmith's Ripley novels and Thomas Harris's later Hannibal Lector books often featured their serial killers in protagonist roles, they were still villains. Lindsay made Dexter a good guy – or at least someone who tried really hard to be good.

Just as Anne Rice influenced *Twilight* and that influenced *Fifty Shades of Grey*, Rice's books were influenced by earlier vampire fiction, but she decided to change the point of view from the vampire hunter to the vampire and found that they had much more interesting lives. A premise Fred Saberhagen also employed in his novel *The Dracula Tape* one year before Rice published *Interview with a Vampire* in 1976.

Changing the POV is such a powerful way to revisit a story, even authors will use it to revisit their own works. Orson Scott Card followed up the hugely popular *Ender's Game* with *Ender's Shadow*, the story of a friend of Ender told at the same time. E.L. James rewrote *Fifty Shades* from the point of view of Mr. Grey.

The existence of both of these books reinforces the point that characters really, really matter. Authors can even openly recycle the same damn plot, but put different people into the story and audiences will pay to find out what happens!

Summing it up: Whether prompted, asking 'What?', twisting things or shifting the POV, you should have no trouble coming up with story ideas if you just start asking your brain questions and see where it leads you.

Try this: Take a story you're familiar with and give it a sideways twist.

Choosing the Right Story

So you've delved deep into your own history, explored the outer reaches of your interests and now you're waiting to find that magical combination that will create the perfect story.

What's the secret to that? I don't know. If you find out, let me know.

I don't know the formula for 'perfect.' However, I do have some thoughts on how to find a good story – or at least one that satisfies my definition of good.

Here are the essential ingredients:

1.) An interesting character

You want someone who is compelling. Not necessarily because of their station in life. A lady billionaire with a private jet might sound fascinating on the surface, but if there's no character to her, then she's just a description. Why should we care about her? What makes her interesting? Does she have an interesting way of looking at the world? Does she solve problems differently than we'd expect?

Bad stories often read like wish-fulfillment. The author just openly describes people they want to be or to fall in love with. Which is less interesting than reading Tinder profiles.

That doesn't mean you can't want to be, or love, your characters, but they have to have more dimension than a cheap plastic Halloween costume.

Your readers have to be just as interested in your characters on page 300 as page 1.

2.) A compelling plot

The plot is what happens. It's your characters + conflicts and the outcome. A good plot keeps you guessing. You don't know what's going to happen next. And when it does, it makes sense.

A good plot generally sounds interesting when you describe it. But a story is so much more than that. There's a reason I put character first. A good character in a weak plot is more enjoyable than a bad character in a great plot.

How do you know when you've found a great character and a great plot? Sometimes you don't know until the book is finished. Even then, it might take time for it to find an audience.

My way to get some indication is to test these ideas on my friends and people I meet.

FRIEND
"What have you been up to?"

ME
"I've been writing a new book."

FRIEND
"Oh really?! What's it about?"

ME
"A Wisconsin farmer who likes to draw pictures of stalks of wheat."

FRIEND
"Uh, huh. Do you know where the bathroom is?"

Clearly this is a fascinating idea for a story. My friend is so excited they have to rush to restroom in order to contain their enthusiasm.

But just to be sure, I should test it out on a few other friends and see if they have the same reaction...

In all seriousness, your friends and people you meet can be a helpful gauge, but they shouldn't be your deciding factor. Nobody can know if it's really a good idea until it's all put together. Even then, the execution of the idea could make or break it.

However, one of the really helpful outcomes of this kind of market testing is that you'll learn how to shape your description and find out how your story will appeal to people in an online world.

Often the only interaction people will have with your story is your Amazon book page. The cover and the description are what will make them buy if the reviews support their impression.

You might lose out on a bunch of wonderful stories because they don't make great elevator pitches, but you can find out which ones will have legs if you try them out at on a few people.

An important key to gauging the marketability of your story is by studying the reaction. **The best response isn't, "That sounds great." It's, "I want to read that."**

Two things to be cautious about:

1.) Your friends might be idiots. If they've never read a book, their opinion as potential book buyers is essentially useless. Unless the mere thought of the existence of your story compels them to get a library card and start taking literature studies classes.

2.) You can go on forever pitching great ideas, one after another. At some point you have to write one. My friends got sick of me pitching ideas. They loved them all. I was told that I should just shut up and write one of them. Any of them. *I did.* And a year later I had my first literary agent and a movie deal. In some alternate universe there's a version of me still trying to come up with the perfect idea. Sucks for him.

Summing it up: Pitching your story in a few sentences can help you gauge people's interest and its potential commercial prospects. But don't spend the rest of your life pitching.

Try this: Take some story ideas you've been struggling with and try to condense them into a pitch. Test them on people and see which ones have traction.

Writer's Lock:

How to start writing your story

Getting Started

Boy, did they love your story idea at the cocktail party last night! Remember the look on the face of that cutie when you explained the book wouldn't be ready for at least a few months and they were all set to buy it on Amazon?

Everyone is as excited about the story as you are! Even the character descriptions have them clinging to your every word. And the fact that the television agents said she could sell that story because your characters will be just as complex and interesting in season eight as the pilot? That's pure gold!

Let's not even talk about how your plot caused and argument as people fought over whether it would make a better movie or HBO series.

You don't need any more proof that you're on top of something magical. Your story is already luring them in and you haven't even started writing it yet.

Um, yeah...About that....

So here you are, sitting in front of your computer, next to stacks of legal pads and notecards filled with details. You've even got a Pinterest board filled with images and cool things to put into your book.

But you can't even write the first word, let alone the first page or chapter.

This is what I call 'Writer's Lock.' It's all there, you just can't figure out how to unleash it.

The source of Writer's Lock is usually one of two things:

1.) You're too nervous and uncertain to start your story.

2.) You have no clue where to begin.

Let me solve #1 for you right now. This is normal. It gets easier with every book you write. And yes, you're going to write more books. This is what writers do. Maybe it's one every couple years. Maybe it's one a month. What matters is that you commit yourself to the idea that you get as many chances to nail it as you like.

Writing isn't like professional sports where if you screw up too often you're out of the game forever. We're not brain surgeons (unless you actually are.) We can have as many failures as we have time for and nobody is going to take away our medical license and sue us for malpractice because we were operating on people in Starbucks.

With writing, you can take as many shots as you want in private and then bury your failures in the backyard next to that annoying neighbor who just wouldn't shut up about how loud you played your stereo.

When someone congratulates me on the reviews a books is (hopefully) getting, I feel like a bad parent that only lets my beautiful children out of the house, while the ugly ones are locked in the basement (FYI: I don't have any children.)

If you have a reasonably good idea that will make a complete story, then write it. If it's just an okay idea, and this is your first book, that's fine. You're going to learn so much in the process that you'll hate yourself if you wait for a better idea the first time out.

I started writing because I thought I had some great ideas for stories. Even to this day, I still haven't even attempted the really good ones because I want to be better writer when I do so. In the meantime, I've written dozens of stories I thought were good enough. Even to this day, I'll write entire novels and shelve them. They weren't a waste of time. I learned something in the process of writing them, but they weren't up to my standard of what I wanted to release.

So just write the thing. A finished bad book is still a book. It means that you're that much closer to the better one.

Let's address #2. This is when you don't know where to begin your story. You're pulling at the leash, ready to go for a run. You're just not sure where to go and how to start.

I experience this all the time. I'm constantly trying to figure out the right entry point into a story.

The good news is that at least you have a story. Some writers are incredibly good at creating captivating beginnings filled with promise, only to never deliver.

I'd rather be stuck with a great story and some uncertainty where to begin than a great start and no real story (this is why I hate writing prompts.)

Here's a simple solution to starting your story: It starts when it gets interesting.

In literature, this is called "The inciting incident." This is the thing that puts the whole story into motion. Your story should begin with this.

An inciting incident can be a slow build or something immediate. I'll explain a little later the three most popular ways to kick that off. For now, you need to think about what sets your story in motion. This should be the event that directly affects your characters, even if they're not present.

Harry Potter and the Sorcerer's Stone starts as Harry's uncle Vernon noticing that some people are acting weird. He's unaware that they're celebrating the end of Voldemort (or so they think.) It's the only time we're not in Harry's presence throughout the entire series. After Dumbledore leaves baby Harry on Vernon's doorstep, the story skips ahead ten years to when Harry is about to be accepted into Hogwarts. The story starts with the inciting incident: Harry's first clash with Voldemort. It then moves on to the next important milestone in Harry's life: Getting accepted to Hogwarts and finding out he's a wizard.

Many classic detective stories start when a client walks into their office. It's such a cliché that modern writers try to avoid that exact scenario. Even though that's how most detectives first encounter their cases (actually it's more often on the phone, but that's less interesting.) A legal thriller can also start with a client stepping into their office.

A frequent alternative to both of those is using the actual event that starts the conflict as the starting point. In that case it would be the murder or the crime that sets the story in motion.

For your story, you want to figure out an interesting entry point that sets the pace for the rest of the novel. If you imagine the dramatic events as points on a graph, find the spot where it's about to start going upwards and begin there.

In the next section I'll explain some of the methods of converting that change into actual structure and plot points. These are different structures you can use that will help launch your novel.

Pro tip: Want to find out how hundreds of great books start? You can find out for free and without having to move from where you're sitting. Just go to Amazon or any other site that sells ebooks and click on the button that will send you a free sample to your reading device. 99% of the time this will be the first chapter or two. You can quickly find out how bestsellers lure their audiences.

Summing it up: Your story starts when the world is about to change for your characters. The longer you take to get to that point, the further away you are from the plot.

Try this: Pick the point in your story where your characters experience their first sudden change. Try to get into that point as quickly as possible, yet still give them some depth.

Starting Structure #1: The Collision

The unshaven man in a moth-eaten black trench coat finished fueling up the rusted El Camino and pulled out of the gas station moments before the police arrived and found the owner slumped over the counter in a puddle of blood.

As his car roared down the highway, the muffler belching bluish smoke, the driver put new bullets into the revolver sitting on his lap, while keeping a careful eye on his rearview mirror.

He stopped only once to check his grease-stained map. Clipped to the corner was a photograph of a middle-aged woman with an uncertain smile and a husband standing next to her, thinking of a better life without her.

Eighty miles away, Belinda Little stared down at the untouched plate of eggs that her husband left behind, curious as to why he was in such a hurry to get to work. Sure, he liked to stay late, or least he told her he did. She knew that he often slipped down to the sports bar to hang out with his work buddies instead of coming home to her. But leaving so early? That was unlike George...

So was the phone call he took late last night when he thought she was sleeping. He sounded almost frantic, his voice rising in anger. Afraid of the cold way he'd been treating her lately, she decided to broach the topic another time.

Belinda nearly forgot about the call when the doorbell rang. When she got up to answer, there was a tall silhouette in the bubble-glass window, blocking the sun, casting a long shadow down the hall and into the middle of her home...

Okay, so this isn't exactly the most inspired bit of writing, but the point is to show you the structure of the "Collision." This is where a story begins with one element about to collide into another.

If the shadow at the door is our gunman from the first scene, then maybe poor Belinda's days are numbered. Or not.

Either way, we see a conflict, the gunman in the El Camino heading straight for our protagonist. Maybe the gunman is a good guy. Maybe she hired him. Who cares. We'll never know. What matters is that the story gets off to a start by showing something is about to happen to someone we're supposed to be interested in.

If this was a novel, we could use a few pages, or even some chapters to give the reader some insight into Belinda's life, maybe even get you to care for her.

By using the collision, we set up a promise to our audience that all the normal stuff is leading somewhere. The more Belinda goes about thinking things are okay, the closer she comes to fate. If she doesn't wake up, bad things are going to happen.

Because it works so well, the collision is one of the most frequently employed techniques in commercial fiction.

There are several different ways you can use a collision at the start of your book. In my example, I told one that's linear. First we meet the gunman, then we meet Belinda, in the exact order that those events happen.

If this was a crime thriller, we might have our bad girl committing some horrific murder up front. When we meet our detective, it's right before she gets called into the case. Rather than a slow build, we jump right into the awfulness so we know what the detective has in store.

Another way you can create a collision is to take a scene from later on in the book and put it up front. This is often used in TV shows to create a sense of, "How did we get here?" This creates a question in the reader's mind and another revelation they'll keep turning the pages to find the answer to.

While it can be an effective method, you run the risk of your audience counting the words until the "interesting" part happens. If you feel compelled to use this technique, it's best to use a scene not too close to the end. Otherwise, the entire book is just one preamble.

Messing around with time is a perfectly legitimate storytelling technique, just be sure that you're not using it to cover up for weak structure and plotting.

Here are some examples of the collision in action:

Jaws: The first scene in Peter Benchley's novel describes the shark attacking a swimmer. This is before we're introduced to Chief Brody. By the time we meet him, we're ready to see how his life is going to be affected by the big fish.

The Godfather: In Mario Puzo's novel, later adapted by Puzo and Francis Ford Coppola into a screenplay, we meet three people at the start of the book, a funeral director wanting revenge, an aging singer who desires a comeback and a shopkeeper trying to keep his daughter's lover in the US. They all have one thing in common – They need the help of Don Corleone.

Before we meet the namesake of the novel, we're shown the influence that he has. Rather than start with a murder or some other trope of a crime story,

Puzo tells his story of the mobster family by showing us the influence and wide-ranging connections.

Jurassic Park: Before we meet our iconic characters, Dr. Grant, Ellie Sattler and Ian Malcolm, Michael Crichton builds the danger they're about to encounter when they finally get to Jurassic Park – something that happens later in the novel. He starts the story with a very clinical description of the InGen controversy, then shows us several possibly dinosaur related encounters from the point of view of a doctor who suspects something nefarious might be taking place on the island.

The danger of the collision is if it's not apparent how the two forces are going to come together, or making it happen much too late. You'll often hear critics talk about being introduced to an antagonist and "Waiting for them to show up." This is a sign that parts before then could be more streamlined.

To recap, here are the three most popular ways to set up a collision:

Prelude: At the start of the story we're introduced to the forces that are going to enter our protagonist's life. A shark eats a swimmer. Three people call upon Don Corleone for help. A doctor realizes those lizard bites didn't come from a lizard.

The Flash forward: We get a glimpse of the state of things later on in the book. In Stephen King's wonderful, *Misery*, we meet Paul Sheldon as he's in some tortured, drugged out state in the hands of the psychotic Annie. We then flashback to his life right before the encounter.

Summing it up: Put the forces that are about to collide front and center at the start of your novel.

Try this: Take a random selection of your favorite books and movies and analyze how the collision is played out. Look at your story and find the points where your character and plot trajectories are starting to veer towards each other. How can you show that at the start of your book?

Starting Structure #2: The Slow Build

Not every story starts with a collision. Sometimes there's a much milder one, or none at all. The story gradually builds towards a point. Arguably, the collision is an essential ingredient in commercial fiction (books that sell well *and* people actually read.) Whereas in literature, which I define as books that are often as much about the prose and writing style as plot and characters, slow builds are part of the world creation.

Some authors enjoy spending time in the minutia before they tell you where the story is going. The goal is to get you invested in the world itself or the mundane. Neither approach is right or wrong. There are audiences that vastly prefer the slow build of lit to the admittedly formulaic pattern of commercial fiction. Often the case is that as an audience becomes more sophisticated (having experienced many books) they crave for the slow build and something that doesn't fit the familiar mold.

The trouble with a slow build is that it can be harder to get your audience onboard. If they're not hooked immediately, they're going to drop off.

If you look at lists of bestselling books and compare it to data that shows you which ones were read all the way through and which ones were abandoned, you'll notice that the buzzed-about great literature is often just collecting dust on people's coffee tables.

Let me reiterate that some of the best writing you'll ever find is in those kinds of books. They just have a more difficult time catching on.

You should write the way you want to write. I love putting in collisions and front-loading my books. The ones I enjoy reading the most do this in a clever way.

Probably the only slow-build books I can recall reading and enjoying, were ones that were pushed upon me by my friends. And that's an important distinction: Commercial fiction sells itself. Lit needs lots of enthusiastic people telling you that it's great.

Summing it up: If you're writing literature, as opposed to commercial fiction, style can be more important than plot.

Try this: If you're having trouble diving into a story, just pick any point and start writing. You might find weaving the tale is more interesting than the final product.

Starting Structure #3: In Medias Res

We've seen the different ways a collision can start your story, and we briefly covered the slow build, another way to begin your book is *in media res*, which is Latin for "in the middle of things." While a collision with a flash-forward or jump to a flashback can be considered *in media res*, I tend to think of those as framing devices.

Sometimes the best way to start a story is right in the middle of a conflict. Using an example from cinema, in the original *Star Wars*, we're dropped right into the story as the Rebel Blockade Runner is being attacked by an Imperial Star Destroyer. The war is already raging. We see the conflict before we even meet our characters.

Unlike a flash-forward scene that then jumps back in time (usually a frustrating thing to have happen in movies), the story launches from there. We get the stakes, we get the universe. It's such a better way to start a movie than a bunch of people sitting around talking about going to war.

Speaking of action, military fiction and spy novels often use *in media res* to start the story. This gives readers a taste of what is in store for them after the set-up of the main characters and conflicts.

One of the most popular examples of this is with James Bond movies. The entire sequence before the opening credits is usually Bond on some mission that may or may not play directly into the plot. This prelude gives you a kind of mini-Bond movie at the start that lets you know after all that slow place-setting as M tells Bond his mission, things are going to get intense.

I think if you can start your story *in media res*, as opposed to a time-shifting framing device, it's usually the better option.

Summing it up: Sometimes it's best to start your story right in the middle of the action.

Try this: Is there some point later on in your story that you could jump right into, instead of the beginning?

Starting Structure #4: Framing Devices

A framing device is basically any narrative method you use to get into your story. It's the story of where the story begins.

In a crime drama, it might be the suspect getting grilled by detectives as he tells them what really happened. In *Citizen Kane*, we meet Kane at the moment of his death and a reporter is tasked with finding out what he meant when he said "Rosebud." While Kane's death was a flash-forward, it set up a framing device of a reporter trying to understand who the man really was.

A framing device can be someone telling you what happened from a historical perspective. They could also be catching you up to where they are at some point later on in the story, like the narrator in *Fight Club*. It's a flash-forward to a flashback that connects at the start of the final act.

Think of a framing device as someone telling you where the story starts, and sometimes meeting up with you at the end to tell you that it's over.

Framing devices are used more frequently than we realize. In *The Big Lebowski*, we all remember Jeff Bridges, The Dude, but part of the glue that holds the story together is the voice of Sam Elliot, as The Stranger.

A framing device gives you a means to start a story wherever you like and have someone catch the reader up to where they should be. You can also use the framing device within your story to call attention to important plot points.

Titanic, one of the most successful movies of all time used a framing device to such great effect that people often forget that it's even there. The bookends and middle connective tissue to the period movie are the scenes onboard a modern exploration ship sending a robotic submarine down to investigate the wreck. They bring an elderly Rose onboard to tell them what really happened.

A framing device should be appropriate to your story. For *Titanic*, putting Rose onboard the exploration ship, telling the crew what really happened, was a natural way to hear her talk about the event and avoided being a generic voice reminiscing from some ethereal perspective. We also got a nice little tie-in to the story at the end when we found out what happened to the necklace.

Summing it up: A framing device is way to set a story within or story or give it context.

Try this: How many framing devices can you recall? *Star Wars* had the opening credits. *Lemony Snicket's A Series of Unfortunate Events* had the narrator: Lemony Snicket.

First Impressions

Every part of your story is important. However, in order to get your readers quickly invested, you need to *hook* them as quickly as possible.

That's why a first sentence (actually the first paragraph) is critical. This is your opening line. Pull it off right, and they want you to tell them more. Bungle it, and you run the risk of them closing the book.

Don't panic! You can go back and rewrite your opening paragraph when you're finished. Sometimes it takes the perspective of a complete book to figure out exactly what you want to say.

Here are some examples from books previously discussed:

Jaws by Peter Benchley:

> The great fish moved silently through the night water, propelled by short sweeps of its crescent tail.

This isn't sophisticated prose. This is storytelling. Benchley tells us there's a very large fish swimming somewhere in the night. We soon find out that this giant is very close to shore.

There's a reason Benchley's book and Spielberg's movie based on Benchley and Carl Gottlieb's screenplay, continues to terrorize millions of people. We don't worry about undertows, jellyfish or skin cancer – more realistic threats to sunbathers. No, we're afraid of sharks in large part because Benchley didn't try to tell the story with an Ishmael-like narrator, like Melville's, *Moby Dick*. Melville wanted to do a character study. Benchley wanted to scare the hell out of us. Both succeeded brilliantly.

The Firm by John Grisham:

> The senior partner studied the résumé for the hundredth time and again found nothing he disliked about Mitchell Y. McDeere, at least not on paper.

Where *Jaws* begins with an introduction to the antagonist in the very first sentence, Grisham's book, *The Firm*, has a slow-building first chapter that hints at the menace to come. Despite the slower pace, the first sentence tells us quite a lot: McDeere is our protagonist. He's applying for a job. He seems well qualified. He's being considered by the highest level of the law firm and they need to know more about him than what's on the page.

By the end of the first chapter you realize that the firm knows far more about McDeere than he realizes and that their methods may not be ones that he would agree to.

Gone Girl by Gillian Flynn:

> When I think of my wife, I always think of her head.

Flynn's he-said, she-wrote story begins with Nick Dunne making a slightly odd observation of his wife. At the close of the first paragraph, he mentions his wife's skull.

For a story about murder, this sets up a certain expectation and preprograms us to think about Nick in a certain way as he goes about explaining things from an otherwise regular guy point of view. All the while, we have in the back of our mind the knowledge that he says some weird things.

I chose these examples quite randomly from a list of best-selling books that were adapted by great filmmakers known for their taste in source material (Sydney Pollack, Steven Spielberg and David Fincher.)

All of these examples are representative of their stories. There's no flowery prose or a affliction of adjectives in the beginning. They show us something plain and simple. They don't tell us how to feel. We're able to figure that out on our own as the story develops.

Jaws starts in the water and much of the book is centered around action taking place there. *The Firm* is largely a book about people in rooms trying to figure out the motives of other people. *Gone Girl* is a story inside people's heads as they analyze their relationship and what's happening in the world around them.

For your first sentence, paragraph and chapter, you want to show people what the rest of the book will be like. Think of it as a promise. You're telling them what kind of story this is going to be and what's going to be important.

Here's a way to look at the start of your book:

First sentence goal: **Grab them.**

First paragraph goal: **Pull them in.**

First chapter goal: **Get them hooked.**

Summing it up: The start of your story is promise to readers of things to come. It sets up the world and what the stakes are going to be.

Try this: Write several imaginary opening lines for novels you haven't mapped out yet.

Writer's Knot:

How to get unstuck in the middle of your story

The Tangle

You're cruising along, fingers flying across the keyboard, the story is just spilling out of you, then you step away for a little while and when you get back...Nothing. You know what's supposed to happen, but it just ain't happening. You're staring at the screen, trying to understand why this river just dried up. What's going on?

I tend to think of this as "Writer's Knot." You're out there in the garden, spraying the begonias, then the water stops. When you go trace the hose back to the faucet you find out that it's all knotted up. Somewhere in that tangled nest is a pinched tube that's stopping it from flowing.

When we're writing we can often find ourselves in the same situation. This is because somewhere, our character arcs, motivations, plot points and background details, things get knotted and we forget what comes next, or we're not sure how to get back into it.

In my personal experience, whenever I've had this problem, I find that the main reason is that I've lost focus. I have my characters going on autopilot, and like some defective Roomba, they've got themselves stuck in the corner, trying to suck up the same patch of tile over and over again.

The fix for this is to step back from your keyboard, literally, and take a long walk, shower, massage or whatever you do to tune out without outside distractions, and get back to basics. You need to ask yourself these questions:

1. What is my conflict?

2. What is my protagonist trying to do?

3. What does my antagonist want?

Every person in your story should have goals. They don't have to be aspirational ones like you hear at a Ms. Universe pageant. However, from the kid who bags your hero's groceries to the villain/romantic interest/natural disaster they're up against, everyone has something they want. Even a rock thrown into the air has a goal – to fall back down.

You need to analyze all the conflicts in your story and how they're addressing the primary one. We often get lost because we took a wrong turn. We started worrying about details that aren't important to the story and sent our characters into a cul-de-sac they can't escape.

The detour may have happened a chapter back and you have to throw it out. Or the problem is in the scene you're currently writing and you have to remind yourself and your characters why everyone is there.

Sometimes the problem isn't that you don't know what happens next. It's that your not as excited to tell it as when you sat down in the beginning. We'll address that in the following chapter...

Summing it up: We often have to step back and take a bird's eye view of things to understand where we are in a story.

Try this: In the middle of a movie or a book, stop and ask yourself how we got to there? What lead the characters to this point? What are the stakes? What was necessary? What wasn't? Those two questions are the make or break between good and bad stories.

Dead Story Walking

What if you analyze your conflicts, checked all your character's motives and everything is where it's supposed to be? In fact, you're spot on where you need to be in your outline, yet it's not moving forward?

I've experienced this. For the longest time it would happen to me at about 70% of my way through a novel. For some reason, everything I'd built just became so overwhelming, I had to put it down and walk away.

After my third novel was abandoned at that point, I decided to do some deep introspection and figure out why I couldn't proceed.

My notecards and outline told me there was a story there and I was certain I had an ending. Yet, for some reason, the muse wasn't musing.

What I realized was that in the middle of telling the story, I forgot to *show* the story. Somewhere along the line, I started dragging the plot forward with a lot of "then this happened." Not literally quite, but the story wasn't unfolding naturally. It was being told. There was no discovery there. Just some guy hammering on a keyboard dictating the events.

At some points it's necessary to move things along this way, but it can start to wear thin when you get bogged down in the minutia and it's just a bunch of exposition.

This is also where your readers run the highest risk of getting pulled out of the story. Everything is just running on rails and they might as well tune out or skip ahead. We've all experience it as readers. We're suddenly half a page ahead and have no idea how we got there.

What's required here are two things:

1. You need to make sure your writing isn't reading like a encyclopedia page. Write so that people are experiencing the story, instead of having it related to them.

Test this by reading sections back to yourself and asking if it feels like you're there or someone is summarizing it for you.

Every important revelation should feel like you're experiencing it and not having it reeled off like a list of bullet points.

71

Remember the most important writing advice: Show me, don't tell me.

2. Find a way to grab them. Treat this like the start of your novel. Maybe this could be a twist, something that changes the circumstances, but it could be also just be paying more attention to your pacing, ensuring that the stakes are laid out fairly well at the start of the scene and you're ending each chapter with a cliffhanger. Try to make your audience ask themselves, "What happens next?!"

You want to make sure that your story is just as full of life in the middle as it is in the beginning. This can be through new insights, fresh characters or a realization that the world has changed.

For a great example of how to make something that could feel played out feel new, check out the films *Groundhog Day* and *The Edge of Tomorrow*. Both are time travel pictures that have to deal with the same situation played over and over again, but they find new life in each scene, giving you something else to think about.

Summing it up: Put yourself in the point of view of the reader. Make sure your story is a sequence of revelations and not a dry list of facts with little meaning.

Try this: Practice finding hooks in the most mundane things. Can you make a trip to Starbucks meaningful?

What if you needed your caffeine for an important meeting? How calamitous would it be if you spilled your drink on your clothes before that important meeting?

Stuck in the DMV

Another form of Writer's Knot is what I call being stuck in the DMV. Things aren't tangled, and you haven't lost sight of your plot, you're just stuck in a plodding part of the story where nothing exciting is happening.

This part of the story might be essential to what's going to happen later on, but right now, it's like sitting through the most boring lecture you can imagine. And you know that if you're bored, your readers are going to fall asleep.

There are several fixes for this:

Skip: Does your story really need this part? Sure, every car chase technically begins with our protagonist learning to drive at some point in her life, but do we need to show the driving test to establish that, yes, she is qualified to take the wheel?

Pre-empt: Sometimes a well-placed sentence in the beginning can save you a boring scene or two. Go back to the start of your story and find out if there's something you can establish early on that will eliminate the need for so much exposition later on.

Truncate: A quick line of dialog can solve a lot of problems – as long as it's not too heavy handed. You see this a lot in bad movies where a character is forced to explain a radical shift in the action. Done well, it can move a story on breezily and the audience is glad that you got to the good parts.

Merge: Is there something else that can be going on at this point? Does you protagonist need to find out all about the dangerous sea life in the coral reef? Could we also have her watching a suspicious person on the charter boat while the marine biologist gives us the important details we'll need later on to appreciate the deadly sea monkey attack?

One of the hallmarks of a great storyteller is the ability to tell several stories at one time. Our hero might be at the dinner table telling her husband about the challenging medical case that was dropped on her lap, while she's also trying to solve her teenage daughter's relationship problems and keep the toddler from spilling his macaroni all over the carpet.

These kinds of scenes work really well. Not just because there's a lot going on, but because we can see that our protagonist's life is very complicated. There's more conflict they have to deal with than just the central premise.

In great storytelling, those little conflicts often dovetail back into the plot. They don't have to, and shouldn't be forced, but they provide a wonderful opportunity to make your character's lives more like our own.

Kill: Stephen King, one of my writing heroes, is know for telling stories with a large cast of characters. What does he do when he gets to the middle of a book and realizes he has too many individual story arcs to resolve? If you've read *The Stand* or *The Dome*, you already know the answer. What G.R.R. Martin likes to do slowly, King does all at once when he murders half his characters mid-story to make room for the chosen ones.

Here's my rule of thumb: **If it feels boring and pedantic to write, it'll feel that way to read.**

You don't need to invent new a crisis and conflict, just take a look around at what's already available. If you step back and examine what you've written so far, assuming your characters and world are complex, there are hundreds of possible conflicts you can bring to the foreground. How do other characters feel about your protagonist's actions? How has the world changed? What threads are there in the beginning that can be resurfaced?

Summing it up: If your story is dragging, try skipping, merging, truncating or murdering to pick up the pace.

Try this: What could you cut out of your story and still have a complete journey? Look for passages that read like Wikipedia entries and try yanking them out.

Step Away from the Keyboard - But Not Too Far

Our brain burns calories and can be overworked like any other part of our body. Sometimes the problem is that we've been running around the same neural pathways over and over and we're beginning to get screen burn like an old school arcade game.

The problem isn't your story. You just need to take a breather and let your brain reset.

Resetting means giving your brain a little down time, NOT jumping onto Facebook or taking yourself down some other rabbit hole. This is the #1 mistake I see writers make.

When they get frustrated, they go to their little comfort zones in search of "likes" or some other distraction. Maybe this will help them solve the problem eventually, but more often than not, it'll take them too far away from what they're trying to solve and make it much harder to get back in. Anybody who has ever been woken out of a really cool dream can attest to how impossible it is to hop right back into the loving arms of whoever was waiting for you in slumberland.

The goal of stepping away is to let you stand back from the chessboard and look at it from a few different angles without the tournament clock counting down, stressing you out.

When I decide to take a break, I take a break from everything. I step away from my computer, turn off my phone and go for a walk. Usually I have the answer in fifteen minutes. That's all it takes. But don't panic if it takes longer. Learning how to solve these problems is a skill like anything else.

If you decide to go find things to put on Pinterest or dive into social media, you'll end up spending a lot more than fifteen minutes solving your problem, in fact, you dramatically increase the likelihood that you'll never return to it.

There's a reason some of the greatest minds enjoyed long walks. It allows us to keep moving, get gently stimulated, but remove us from every other problem in the world that's waiting for us.

I'm such a big fan of the walk, I can point to the spots where I solved one problem or another. Most of my best writing happens when I'm not actually writing.

ANDREW MAYNE

Summing it up: Sometimes we have Writer's Block because or brain just needs a rest – but not a distraction.

Try this: Find more time for walks in your writing process.

Rethink Your Ending

Another cause of Writer's Knot is uncertainty about how to end your story. The tidy little conclusion that you envisioned when you started to write, isn't so tidy anymore.

This, oddly enough, is a good thing. It means your story is more complex than you imagined and that your readers we'll be just as interested to see how it gets resolved as you are.

The solution is to step back, look at your unresolved conflicts and figure out how they can be solved in a way that suits the story. Sometimes you can kill two birds with one stone and resolve one thread with another.

Part of the reason I had trouble finishing some of my earlier novels was that I knew the ending was supposed to be drawing near, but I still felt like I was a long ways away. Through sheer effort and forcing myself through, I realized that the resolution often wasn't as far off as I feared. In the cases where it was far off, I could make it happen sooner after I did a rewrite and excised the parts that were dragging on my story.

Don't walk away from your story when things get complicated. Stick to basics: What was your conflict? How is it resolved? The way your protagonist solves the problem at the end of the book should be different than how they would have at the start. That's what all the stuff in the middle is for – showing us how they adapted.

You as a writer have to adapt too. As your story gets its own life and the universe you've created takes on dimension, you should reconsider how the resolution works out in this more fully-realized world.

Summing it up: It's better to resolve a story that's complicated than one that's too linear.

Try this: Come up with as many different alternatives you can. Choose the one that best suits the tone and premise at the beginning of the novel.

Finally

Whenever I participate on writing panels and someone from the audience asks about writer's block, the answer from the other writers is almost universally that it doesn't exist. They treat the notion like a UFO sighting, something with which they have absolutely no experience.

Maybe they're telling the truth. Maybe they're acting like superstitious ball players who don't want to jinx themselves by admitting that it's a real thing, lest they turn around and see Writer's Block hovering over their shoulder.

What I do know is that I've stared at blank pages, searching for ideas. I've sat in front of keyboards, with my fingers frozen. I've been in the middle of books, feeling like I was adrift, and land nowhere in sight.

While I'll say that I've never found myself at a loss for words, it's the *right* ones that eluded me.

I think the difference between myself and the other writers is that I'm much newer at the game. I've been writing all my life, but I've only had the pressure of writing novels with any kind of frequency in the last few years.

Where they have decades of experience sitting in front of their keyboards, the memory of what it's like to be starting out is still very fresh in my mind. I've always had ideas, but not the knowledge of how to shape them into narratives.

This knowledge comes from experience. Like many experiences, it can be so difficult to pin down when and were it was acquired, it's easy to assume you've always known.

As we saw at the start of this book, you've always been a storyteller. It's in your genes. The challenge is controlling it and being able to call upon that ability at will.

I hope that this guide has given you some direction and insight into the different situations that we collectively call "Writer's Block." Hopefully, as you break through and find the stories you want to tell and understand how to navigate the barriers, Writer's Block will become a fading memory to the point when you're on a writing panel and someone asks you about it, you'll too will be able to reply with certainty that it doesn't exist.

One more thing: I've included 50 creativity boosters you can try whenever you find yourself stuck or need a little inspiration.

50 Creativity Boosters

Here's a list of 50 things you can try to boost your creativity. Some are as simple as watching a movie and rewriting the ending. Others are a little more involved and require you to step outside into that place writer's traditionally try to avoid called "The World."

1. Take a character from one book or movie and imagine what would happen if you transplanted them into a different story entirely. This could be comedic: Forrest Gump in *Silence of the Lambs*, or serious, Jack Reacher in *The Godfather*.

2. Have a conversation with a stranger. Next time you're at a restaurant or in a long line, talk to the person nearest to you and do a little mini-interview. This may feel weird, but you never know what may turn up. I've learned nuclear secrets, strange family histories and totally not-true but fascinating information doing this.

3. Mash-up a book or a movie. What would *Fight Club* meets *Star Wars* be like? How about *The Girl With the Dragon Tattoo* plus *The Hunger Games*? An original combination is an original idea if it has its own life.

4. Walk through a book store and try to imagine the stories based solely on the book covers. Were you close to the description? Did you come up with some other wildly different idea?

5. Listen to a movie soundtrack as you walk and try to imagine the scene that should go along with the music.

6. Imagine people you know were the characters in a popular book. What would happen if your family had to take the great trip west in *The Grapes of Wrath*?

7. Read random Ask Me Anything discussions on Reddit. I've read stories of what it's like to go to county jail, be a CEO of a billion-dollar company and how someone tells their family they have a terminal illness. Some of the most touching things I've ever read has been from non-writers sharing their world with others.

8. Take a trip through your phone's photo album and examine all the photos you've taken. What are some details you never noticed? What do the photos say about the photographer?

9. Next time you're out, take photos of everything. Start building an album of photos you can take inspiration from. Capture the little things; chairs in a room, the paintings on a restaurant wall, the way people are dressed. Use your phone as a filing cabinet of details.

10. Who is an interesting character in a story that you think deserved more attention? Is there a story waiting to be told about them? In *Wicked*, Gregory Maguire decided that the Wicked Witch of the West needed her own story.

11. Go to a historical attractions and ask lots of questions. Get the tour guides talking. Find out the history behind the displays.

12. Visit your local historical society and find out the history of where you live. Even the smallest town has its sordid secrets.

13. Imagine sequels that never happened. Sometimes things get more interesting after the first story. Once characters have been introduced and world is created, you can start telling more complex stories without having to spend your time setting the scene.

14. Watch a movie you've never seen on mute. What do you think it's about? What do you imagine the characters are saying? You'd be surprised at how spot on and far off you might be.

15. Give your casual acquaintances a secret life you don't know about. Does the woman who delivers your mail ride with a biker club on the weekends (mine did!). What does the clerk at the supermarket do at night? Argue with his wife? Play board games?

16. Take some old magazines, cut out the photos, mix them up and see what kind of stories you can tell from them. This works best with National Geographic and magazines that feature more than models and car ads.

17. What if your favorite character was actually a villain? How dangerous would Jason Bourne be if he decided to go evil?

18. What if your favorite villain was good? How could you justify the extreme behavior of Annie Wilkes in *Misery*? Not just explain, but make them heroic? It's important to remember that bad people often see themselves as the hero in their own story.

19. Pour yourself a beverage, sit in front of your computer and use Google Street View to take a trip to a foreign city or to investigate a neighborhood in another state. Use the arrows to advance block by block and make note of everything that stands out, like you're an anthropologist.

20. Pick up a non-fiction memoir or historical book and read about the life of a living person. Make

notes about things you could use to embellish a fictional character.

21. Start a book by writing the last chapter. Where do you want it to land? What do you want to be your biggest emotional impact? Then start writing your book with that pivotal moment in mind.

22. Look around you. What books are sitting on your shelves? What objects are near you? What do they say about the kind of stories you should be writing?

23. Pick up a book you started reading and couldn't finish. How would you have made it different? Where did it lose your interest?

24. Take a walk through a different part of town. Who lives in these houses? What are their stories? At the risk of sounding creepy, sometimes I take long drives at night and think about these things.

25. Pick up one of your favorite novels and a highlighter. Go through the book and circle interesting sections. Look for points where the stakes were raised, conflicts are introduced and how much time is spent on characters you loved.

26. Examine a crime story in the newspaper and try to imagine how everything got to that point. What was the bank robber doing earlier in the

day? What was the bank teller worrying about before the hold up?

27. Go sit in court for a day. Listen to the different cases, watch how the attorneys try to make their arguments for and against. Pay attention to who is in the audience watching.

28. Talk to cops. They have great stories. Cops see more crazy stuff in one night than most of us do our entire life.

29. Look at MeetUp.com for a random group that sounds interesting to you. You don't have to join, but you never know what you might learn from a club of model railroad engineers or spelunkers.

30. Read an obituary. How was this person's life summed up? What did their loved ones think it was important to tell the world?

31. Eavesdrop. If someone is talking a little too loudly, then by all means listen. What's their personal drama? How can you use this loudmouth in a story?

32. In the 1920's the Dadaists had a technique of cutting up text and rearranging the words to create new works. William S. Burroughs popularized this method after being introduced to it by Brion Gysin. You can use this to create very random, yet sometimes interesting starting points.

33. Keep a journal of random quotes, lines and anything else you find interesting. It could be stream of consciousness or a variations on a theme.

34. Take a trip through the personal ads on Craigslist and see how people are presenting themselves. What are they looking for? What are they projecting?

35. Ask strangers what their favorite books are. You might be surprised at what they tell you. It might be a classic, or a book that they found in a difficult time in their life. Often, the story of how they found the book is just as important as the book itself.

36. Watch a movie with a smart friend and break down what happened and why. Find out why you liked or didn't like certain parts and vice versa.

37. Make a list of your favorite authors and try to figure out what makes them unique and why you like them. What can you learn from them?

38. Watch the most random documentary you can find on Netflix. Search for inspiration in places you would never normally think to look.

39. Create a text message conversation between two characters. What do they talk about when they don't have to be interesting?

40. Visit a home for retired people. Find out their stories. Stephen Ambrose wrote *Band of Brothers* based on the recollections of the men who served in Easy Company during World War II.

41. Go to a city council meeting. Most of it will be mind numbing, but you'll find out what the hot-button topics are in your community and meet some very interesting characters.

42. Go to a garage sale and look through the items. What stories do they tell you?

43. Make up biographies and backstories for complete strangers.

44. Try to sum your friends up single-sentence character descriptions. Don't show this to them if you want to keep them as friends.

45. Write alternative first sentences for your favorite novels.

46. Take a look at your life and try to imagine where you would be if you'd made different choices. What are you doing in an alternate universe?

47. Write a "extra" scene for one of your favorite movies. Maybe this would help the story or give added insight into the characters.

48. Try your hand at writing two-sentence stories. This is a great way to prime your brain for conflict. Here's an example: *He always stops crying when I pour the milk on his cereal. I just have to remember not to let him see his face on the carton.*

49. Make a list of your favorite books and movies and try creating wild mash-ups.

50. Take an improv class.

Author thanks

I hope you found something useful here. If so, I'd love it if you wrote a blurb on Amazon or Goodreads. I can't tell you how much this means to me when someone takes the time to do that.

If you'd like to keep up to date with what I'm up to and my future projects, please sign up for me email list at AndrewMayne.com.

You can follow me online at:
Twitter.com/AndrewMayne
Facebook.com/AndrewMayne

I also have lots of videos about writing and other topics at: YouTube.com/AndrewMayne and I do a weekly podcast on creativity that can be found at WeirdThings.com.

Thank you for reading this!

Best,

Andrew Mayne
@AndrewMayne

Also by Andrew Mayne

How to Write a Novella in 24 Hours
Station Breaker
Game Knight
Public Enemy Zero
The Grendel's Shadow
Hollywood Pharaohs
Knight School

Jessica Blackwood:
Angel Killer
Name of the Devil

The Chronological Man:
Monster in the Mist
The Martian Emperor

Made in the USA
Columbia, SC
11 July 2020

12932945R00057